G is for Ghana

G is for Ghana

ISBN: 978-9988-8808-8-0

Published by Smartline Ltd, January 2020

Copyright 2019 © Text, Fatima Subri-Smith
Published by Smartline Limited,
DTD C3 Coastal Estates,
Baatsona, Spintex-Road,
Accra, Ghana.
Website: www.smartlinepublishers.com
Email: info@smartlinepublishers.com

All rights reserved. No part of this publication may be reproduced, stored in a retrieval system or transmitted in any form or by any means, electronic, mechanical, photocopying, recording or otherwise, without the prior permission of Smartline Limited.

SMARTLINE

G is for Ghana

Fatima Subri-Smith

A is for ***Akwaaba***. In the Ghanaian language, Twi , akwaaba means welcome. In Ghana, guests are very important and must be welcomed properly and warmly. After an embrace or handshake, it is important to offer water to the guests, whether they are thirsty or not!

A is for *Ampe*, a game played mostly by girls. The number of players ranges from 2 to 12 children. This fun game is played by jumping, clapping hands and the lifting of a leg at the same time. Ampe helps with one's coordination and agility. It is a great sport for physical education (P.E.) too.

Bb

B is for **Bragoro**, a rite performed for girls in the Akan tribe when they reach puberty. The Krobo tribe calls this event Dipo. This special occasion is celebrated with girls dressed up in beautiful traditional costumes. Family and elders of the community gather and a special dish, called eto with boiled eggs, is prepared for the girls and fed to them. It is a very happy time with lots of singing and dancing.

B is for **Black Stars**, Ghana's national football team. It was founded around 1920 and played as a team in the then Gold Coast. Children, especially boys, start playing football almost as soon as they can walk, and they all dream of playing for the Black Stars one day! Some famous past and present Black Stars players include Abedi Pele and Asamoah Gyan. Most Ghanaians are very proud of the national team especially when they play in the World Cup.

Cc

C is for ***Cedi***, Ghana's currency. The word cedi means cowry shells in the Akan language. A long time ago, cowry shells were used instead of money. Later on, pounds, shillings and pence were introduced by the British until 1965 when it was changed to the cedi. If you looked closely, you would see the face of the once famous Ashanti Queen, Yaa Asantewaa, hidden in the cedi note as a watermark.

C is for ***Coal Pot***. This traditional stove can be found in almost every home. Ghanaians cook most dishes on the coal pot. It is made of iron, has a bowl or trapezium-shaped opening on top which is filled with charcoal, and is lit with kerosene and matches.

Dd

D is for Akosombo ***Dam***, a man-made dam built from 1961 to 1965, and is situated on the Volta River in south-eastern Ghana. The dam provides electricity to most parts of Ghana and some neighbouring countries. It is surrounded by beautiful woodlands and hills, an amazing landmark that attracts a lot of tourists.

D is for ***Damii*** (also known as draughts), a game played mostly by men in towns and villages on verandas and under trees. It is a board game with chequered patterns. It is played by moving the squared and circular wooden pieces across the board at a fast pace. Damii is very popular and is played with a lot of passion.

Ee

E is for *Education* which is valued and enjoyed by Ghanaians, both young and old. Children usually start school from about age six. There are also kindergarten provisions for children in urban towns and cities. Children who attend state schools wear the same uniform all over the country.

E is for *English*, which is the official language spoken in Ghana by about 70 percent of the population. There are, however, so many Ghanaian languages and dialects spoken in the country as well. The Gold Coast, now Ghana, was ruled by the British for a long time. They were the first people to set up formal schools in the Gold Coast until 1957 when she achieved her independence. Many people who have not been to school speak a form of English known as 'Pidgin English'.

Ff

F is for *Festivals*, a colourful and vibrant part of Ghanaian culture. Ghana has many different cultural groups called tribes, and each has its own unique language and traditions. These tribes hold special festivals in different months of the year. It is a time to get together, eat, dance, and celebrate their cultural heritage.

F is for *Fishing*, which is mostly done by men who live in the coastal towns and villages. It is the main source of income for these people and, most often, skills are passed down from father to son. Fishermen bring in their catch to the beach, where fishmongers buy the fish and sell in the markets.

Gg

G is for ***Ghana***, a small country in West Africa with different landscapes – from savannah plains in the north, to mountains and rainforest in the south. There are about 79 different languages and dialects spoken, and each tribe has its own culture and cuisine. This makes Ghana one of the most exciting countries in West Africa for food lovers. The weather is as warm as its people, and Ghanaians are well known for their hospitality.

G is for *Gome* dance. It is one of the traditional dances of the Ga tribe in the south-eastern part of Ghana, around Accra. This special dance is usually performed during Ga festivals and celebrations such as Homowo.

Hh

H is for ***Hoe***, a unique hand farming tool widely used to clear weeds, dig the ground, scrape the earth, loosen the soil and a lot more! It is locally made by blacksmiths. A hoe has a long wooden handle and a flat iron or steel blade attached to it at a right angle. Even though it is a valuable tool, working with it is backbreaking.

H is for ***Homes*** which come in all shapes, sizes and colours! Homes in Ghana range from small huts in the villages to large mansions in the cities. Many Ghanaian children live in large families which may consist of their parents, brothers and sisters, a grandparent or two, some cousins, aunties and uncles, all in one big home or compound! They live this way to help, support and take care of each other.

Ii

I is for **Industry** which is essential for the country to grow and take care of its citizens. Ghana imports a lot of the things its people use on a daily basis, but always strives to produce more items locally. These include food, drinks, clothes, footwear, medicines and household appliances. Ghana exports goods like gold, cocoa and timber.

I is for ***Independence*** Day of Ghana, which used to be a British Crown Colony known as the Gold Coast. This name was adopted by the British because earlier Portuguese explorers and traders had discovered so much gold between the rivers Ankobra and the Volta. Osagyefo Dr Kwame Nkrumah was the one who led the Gold Coast to independence on 6th March, 1957 and that was when he changed the name from Gold Coast to Ghana. On that day, Osagyefo gave a very powerful speech which includes the famous sentence, "Ghana, our beloved country, is free forever!" An amazing Independence Arch in the largest public square was built to remind Ghanaians of this momentous occasion. It is now used for national parades and celebrations.

Jj

J is for **Jollof rice**, a hugely popular dish in Ghana. It is made by cooking rice in rich and spicy tomato stew. Most people add meat (especially chicken) for extra flavour. Jollof rice is usually cooked for special occasions like parties, weddings and other celebrations. It is absolutely delicious and is loved by all.

J is for ***James Fort***, which was built by the British in 1673. It is one of the smaller forts built along the coast by the Europeans who first came to Ghana. There are other forts and castles along the southern coast of Ghana– One of the largest is the Elmina Castle which was used to keep slaves before they departed the shores of Ghana. A lighthouse was built at James Fort in 1871. Today, the area around the fort is known as Jamestown and has become a vibrant and interesting part of the capital, Accra.

Kk

K is for ***Kente*** a multi-coloured fabric worn mostly by people from the Akan tribe. Kente is woven in a little town in the Ashanti region of Ghana called Bonwire. This beautiful fabric is usually sewn into elegant outfits which are worn on special occasions and during celebrations.

K is for **Kaya**, meaning porter. Nowadays, these kayas are mostly young boys and girls based in open markets and supermarkets in city centres. Their role is to carry groceries in baskets or pans on their heads, follow shoppers throughout the shopping trip to help them with their load. They are paid a small amount for their services.

Ll

L is for ***Larabanga Mosque***, said to be the oldest mosque in Ghana. Larabanga is in the northern part of Ghana. Some believe this mosque was built by God and is home to a very old Holy Quran (the holy book for Muslims), which is also believed to have descended from heaven. The Larabanga Mosque is now a popular tourist site.

L is for **Labadi Beach**, a very popular beach in Accra. Many people like to visit this beach on weekends and public holidays with their friends and families. Labadi Beach is a good place for relaxing and enjoying entertaining activities such as acrobatic performances, live music and barbeques. It is also well known for its spicy kebabs.

Mm

M is for the **Monkey Sanctuary** in Boabeng-Fiema in the Brong Ahafo Region of Ghana. This is home to two different species of monkeys–the Mona and Columbus. These monkeys are special because they are so friendly that people can get close to them and feed them. The sanctuary is in a large forest which has unusual trees and birds.

M is for **Makola**, a sprawling market in the heart of Accra, the capital of Ghana. It is one of the largest and oldest open markets in the country. There are wholesalers as well as retailers selling in little stalls and even on tabletops. The wares range from vegetables and spices to colourful African fabrics, and from mouth-watering fresh and smoked fish to dazzling beads and other jewellery. There is often heavy traffic around Makola. It is open market where you can find everything you need, as long as you know where to look.

Nn

N is for *Naming Ceremony*, usually performed on the 8th day of a baby's life. Family and friends gather together, and the parents announce the name they have chosen for the baby. Babies in Ghana are often given the name of the day on which they were born. Special rituals are performed, usually by an older family member to welcome the baby into the world.

N is for ***Nkuto*** (shea butter). It is a solid fat extracted from the nuts of the shea butter tree. Nkuto looks like whipped cream and is used widely as a skin moisturiser, hair cream, and also for cooking in the northern part of Ghana, where the tree grows in abundance.

Oo

O is for **Ol'man and O'lady** (Old Man and Old Lady), affectionate terms used for grandparents and old people in the community. Old people are considered wise and are admired and respected. They teach young people the customs and traditions of their tribes, and often tell the little children fascinating stories, myths and legends.

O is for *Otumfuo*, a title given to the king of the Ashanti Kingdom, the largest and most powerful kingdom in Ghana. He is popularly known as Asantehene, the king of the Asantes. The Asantehene is highly respected by most chiefs and people in Ghana. On special occasions, Otumfuo adorns himself in gold and sits on a special seat known as the Sika Agua (the Golden Stool) to greet his subjects. This special stool is solely made of gold and legend has it that the great fetish priest Okomfo Anokye, called it from the skies.

Pp

P is for ***Pottery.*** In Ghana, clay that is used for making pots is dug from river banks. There are clay pots in most Ghanaian homes, and they are used for cooking, storing water, grinding and as items of decoration. These pots are mostly made by women in villages and small towns while sitting under shady trees or in the communal yard.

P is for **Piggyback**, the most popular way for mothers to carry babies around. Usually, the baby lies on the mother's back on his/her stomach, and a cloth is tied tightly over the baby's back and around the mother. This leaves the mother's hands free to do her chores while keeping the baby safe at the same time.

Qq

Q is for ***Queen Mother***. A long time ago, there used to be lots of powerful kings and queens in Ghana. Yaa Asantewaa was the famous Queen Mother of Ejisu, a town near Kumasi in Ashanti. She led a large army to fight the British who had exiled a powerful Ashanti king. She is still remembered and respected as one of the bravest women that ever lived in Ghana.

Q is for ***Quahu*** (traditionally spelt Kwahu) Mountains, which stand about 2,500 feet above sea level. The road leading to the top of the mountain winds along the edge of steep slopes and cliffs. Visitors can stroll along paths under the forest to admire the numerous tropical tree species. Colourful butterflies flip along the edges of the forest. An observation point on the mountaintop offers a most spectacular view to which few sights can compare!

Rr

R is for ***River Volta***, the largest and longest river in Ghana. Together with its three main tributaries, this beautiful river flows through all parts of the country from the North to the South. River Volta is a means of livelihood for most people who live along it, as it gives its people fertile land to farm and a place to fish. Dotted along its banks are a number of scenic beaches and interesting flora and fauna. The River Volta is also an important source of hydro-electric power (electricity) and drinking water.

R is for **Rainforests**, one of which can be found at Kakum National Park in the Central Region of Ghana. Besides the plant and highly developed bird world, this rainforest is also home to the endangered mona-meerkat monkey, pygmy elephant and forest buffalo. A suspension bridge, about 30m above the forest floor, has been built as a walkway for visitors to catch the best glimpse of the rainforest.

Ss

S is for **Symbols**. In Ghana, clans have symbols and so does the nation. Each symbol stands for something very important to the people. The most popular ones are the Adinkra symbols. The word Adinkra means farewell. Originally, these symbols were printed on fabrics which were made into robes worn by tribal chiefs to funerals. These days, the symbols can still be found on Ghanaian fabrics, as well as artefacts.

S is for ***Sweet, Juicy Sugarcane*** which is often chewed for its juice or as a snack. Sugarcane, a key ingredient in making sugar, is a tall, tree-like bamboo. In Ghana, it is usually sold on the streets all over the cities, towns and villages.

Tt

T is for **Tuo Zaafi** (aka TZ). Zaafi is an expression in Hausa language which means 'very hot'. 'TZ' is a thick porridge-like Hausa dish made from dry corn flour cooked in boiling water. It is eaten by tearing off a piece of the cooked corn flour by hand, and dipping it into a thick soup usually made of okra. This delicious dish is very popular, especially in the northern part of Ghana.

T is for ***Tro-tro***, a crowded, but efficient and inexpensive means of transport in a minibus used for short distance travel. It evolved from the Ga word tro (meaning three pence), which was the fare at the time when Ghana was still known as the Gold Coast. Most tro-tro minibuses have interesting signs and sayings, or words of wisdom written across them; they still remain a popular means of transport.

Uu

U is for ***Kwame Nkrumah University of Science and Technology*** in Kumasi in the Ashanti Region. It is named after Osagyefo Dr. Kwame Nkrumah, who became the first president of Ghana in 1957. This university is one of the first three universities in Ghana, and is well known for research and training in Science and Technology.

U is for *Ceremonial Umbrellas* used by chiefs and queen mothers during festivals and other important ceremonies. The chiefs, queen mothers and other important guests sit underneath these huge, brightly-coloured ceremonial umbrellas during such events.

Vv

V is for **Vulture**, a bird disliked and shunned in Ghana, because vultures feed from rubbish dumps, and eat rotten food and dead animals. In the villages, where chickens are kept in the backyards, vultures often prey on the young chicks: they swoop on these chicks and eat them. Vultures are also sometimes considered a bad omen.

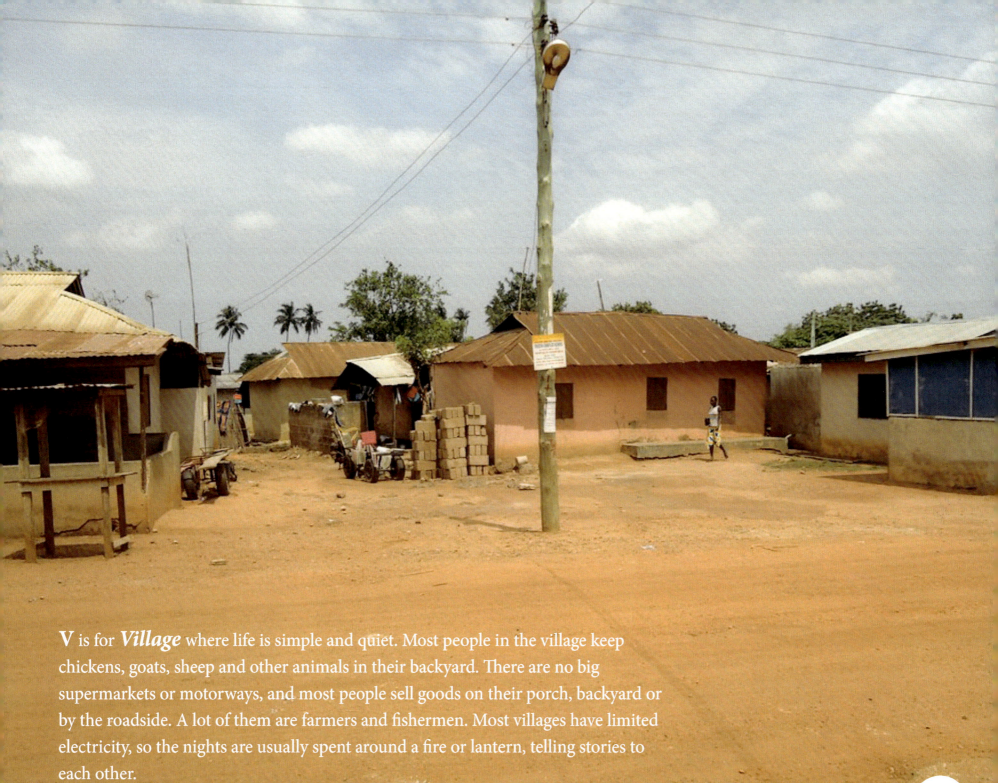

V is for ***Village*** where life is simple and quiet. Most people in the village keep chickens, goats, sheep and other animals in their backyard. There are no big supermarkets or motorways, and most people sell goods on their porch, backyard or by the roadside. A lot of them are farmers and fishermen. Most villages have limited electricity, so the nights are usually spent around a fire or lantern, telling stories to each other.

Ww

W is for *Weaving Bolga* (short for Bolgatanga) baskets in the northern part of Ghana. These baskets are woven by indigenous people from the historical town of Bolgatanga, which means clayey, rocky land. Weaving has long been a traditional skill here, and these baskets are woven mostly by women. They use straw from elephant grass which grows along the banks of rivers in the area. The straw is then dyed and woven into colourful baskets.

W is for *Washing* by the riverside, a popular way for children to have a bath, mostly in the villages. The adults, especially the women, go down to the river to wash pots or clothes by hand. In Ghana, very few people own or use washing machines. Therefore, people hand wash clothes in buckets or large basins.

Xx

X is for *Xɔse* (pronounced /hɔsè/). In the Ghanaian language, Ewe (pronounced /ewè/), xɔse means belief or faith. Apart from religious belief or faith, Ghanaians from all parts of the country place great value on self-belief or faith in oneself. This is as a result of our great history, cultural heritage and the mighty achievements of our forefathers. Details of all these are passed down from one generation to the next by word of mouth or in Social Studies lessons in basic schools. Right from a very early age, children are encouraged to be bold, believe in themselves, dream big and determine to accomplish more than their parents have done.
confidently in class room setting.

X is for the Ghanaian ***Xylophone***, also known as gyli. This fine traditional musical instrument is mainly played by the Dagara people from the Upper West and Northern Regions of Ghana. The xylophone is made of different lengths of wood arranged and tied together with two strings, all sitting on top of a number of gourds. The Xylophone or Gyli is played with two mallets (drumsticks which have rounded rubber heads) to produce a beautiful melody. The most famous xylophonist in Ghana is Aaron Bebe Sukura.

Yy

Y is for *Yams*, a root vegetable much like potatoes, only much bigger and longer. Yams are eaten in almost every household in Ghana. There are many different types of yam, each one with a distinct flavour. The most popular is the puna. Yams can be boiled, fried, roasted or mashed. Whichever way it is cooked, it tastes absolutely yummy!

Y is for ***Yapei Queen Boat***, a ferry boat which plies the Volta River from Akosombo in the south, all the way to Yeji in the north-eastern part of the Brong Ahafo Region. This ferry is therefore essential in linking the northern and southern parts of the country. It is primarily a cargo vessel, but has limited cabin and deck spaces for passengers. Of all the boats in Ghana, the MV Yapei Queen travels the longest route, and is very popular with adventurous travellers.

Zz

Z is for **Zomi** (also spelt somi), a type of vegetable oil made from palm fruit. It is seasoned with some special herbs, giving it a sweet aroma. Zomi is widely eaten in the southern part of Ghana and is used to cook kontomire (spinach) sauce. Zomi is to kontomire as olive oil is to pasta sauce. This palm oil is known to be rich in beta-carotene and also fatty acids which promote growth.

Z is for ***Zaina Lodge***, a hotel at the Mole National Park near Damango in the Northern Region. There is a range of wildlife such as elephants, monkeys, baboons, warthogs, antelopes and bushbucks at this safari park. Visitors and tourists staying here have the opportunity to see such wildlife bathing in ponds close by, and also experience open-top Toyota land cruiser tours close to the animals.

Word List

A   is for *Akwaaba*

A   is for *Ampe*

B   is for *Bragoro*

B   is for *Black Stars*

C   is for *Cedi*

C   is for *Coal pot*

D   is for Akosombo *Dam*

D   is for *Damii*

E   is for *Education*

E   is for *English*

F   is for *Festival*

F   is for *Fishing*

G   is for *Ghana*

G   is for *Gome dance*

H   is for *Hoe*

H   is for *Homes*

I   is for *Industry*

I   is for *Independence Day*

J   is for *Jollof rice*

J   is for *James Fort*

K   is for *Kente*

K   is for *Kaya*

L   is for *Larabanga Mosque*

L   is for *Labadi Beach*

M   is for *Monkey*

M   is for *Mole National Park*

N   is for *Naming Ceremony*

N   is for *Nkuto*

O   is for *Ol'man* and *O'lady*

O   is for *Otumfuo*

P   is for *Pottery*

P   is for *Piggyback*

Q   is for *Queen Mother*

Q   is for *Quahu* (traditionally spelt Kwahu)

R   is for *River Volta*

R   is for *Rainforests*

S   is for *Symbols*

S   is for Sweet, juicy *sugarcane*

T   is for *Tuo zaafi*

T   is for *Tro-tro*

U   is for Kwame Nkrumah *University* of Science and Technology

U   is for Ceremonial *umbrellas*
V   is for *Vulture*
V   is for *Village*
W   is for *Weaving*
W   is for Washing
X   is for *Xylophone* (gyli)
X   is for *Xɔse*
Y   is for *Yam*
Y   is for *Yapei Queen*
Z   is for *Zomi* (also spelt somi)
Z   is for *Zaina Lodge*

GLOSSARY

1. Adventurous
2. Agility
3. Appliance
4. Artifacts
5. Ashanti
6. Backbreaking
7. Blacksmiths
8. Cargo
9. Coordination
10. Cuisine
11. Cultural Heritage
12. Dam
13. Dazzling
14. Dialects
15. Fauna
16. Fertile
17. Festivals
18. Fetish priest
19. Indigenous
20. Kebabs
21. Kerosene
22. Kindergarten provisions
23. Lighthouse
24. Melody
25. Moisturizer
26. Omen
27. Osagyefo
28. Outfits
29. Portuguese
30. Puberty
31. Retailers
32. Rite
33. Safari
34. Sanctuary
35. Spectacular
36. Sprawling
37. Symbols
38. Trapezium
39. Vibrant
40. Watermark

ACKNOWLEDGEMENTS

To my husband, thank you for supporting me. Zara, my daughter, your unfaltering support, encouragement, and belief in this book were most appreciated in times when I didn't have the urge to write.

Marian, I cannot thank you enough for your contribution.
To my parents, this book is in your honour.